Extreme Stars!

Q&A

Smithsonian | Collins

An Imprint of HarperCollins Publishers

Smithsonian Mission Statement

For more than 160 years, the Smithsonian has remained true to its mission, "the increase and diffusion of knowledge." Today the Smithsonian is not only the world's largest provider of museum experiences supported by authoritative scholarship in science, history, and the arts but also an international leader in scientific research and exploration. The Smithsonian offers the world a picture of America, and America a picture of the world.

Special thanks to Roger Launius, Historian, National Air and Space Museum, Smithsonian Institution, for his invaluable contribution to this book.

This book was created by **jacob packaged goods LLC** (www.jpgglobal.com):
Written by: Sarah L. Thomson
Creative: Ellen Jacob, Kirk Cheyfitz, Carolyn Jackson, Sherry Williams, Dawn Camner

On the cover: This huge gas cloud, or nebula, is located in galaxy M33. Inside the cloud, stars are being born.

Photo credits: title page: A. Caulet (ST-ECF, ESA) and NASA; **credits page:** NASA, ESA, and The Hubble Heritage Team (STScI/AURA); **contents page:** NASA, H. Ford (JHU), G. Illingworth (UCSC/LO), M.Clampin (STScI), G. Hartig (STScI), the ACS Science Team, and ESA; **pages 4–5:** NASA and The Hubble Heritage Team (STScI/AURA); **page 5, inset:** Solar & Heliospheric Observatory (SOHO). SOHO is a project of international cooperation between ESA and NASA; **pages 6–7:** Solar & Heliospheric Observatory (SOHO). SOHO is a project of international cooperation between ESA and NASA; **page 8, inset:** NASA, H. Ford (JHU), G. Illingworth (UCSC/LO), M.Clampin (STScI), G. Hartig (STScI), the ACS Science Team, and ESA; **pages 8–9:** A. Caulet (ST-ECF, ESA) and NASA; **page 10:** top left: The Hubble Heritage Team (AURA/STScI/NASA); bottom left: NASA and H. Richer (University of British Columbia); **pages 10–11:** NASA, ESA, and The Hubble Heritage Team (STScI/AURA); **page 11, inset:** Jon Morse (University of Colorado), and NASA; **pages 12–13:** NASA, ESA, and The Hubble Heritage Team (STScI/AURA); **page 14:** NASA and ESA; **page 15:** J. P. Harrington and K. J. Borkowski (University of Maryland), and NASA; **pages 16–17:** NASA, ESA and The Hubble Heritage Team (STScI/AURA); **page 17, inset:** L. Ferrarese (Johns Hopkins University) and NASA; **page 18:** bottom left: NASA; **pages 18–19:** NASA/JPL-Caltech/N. Smith (Univ. of Colorado at Boulder); **page 20, inset:** NASA, ESA, The Hubble Heritage Team (STScI/AURA), J. Bell (Cornell University) and M. Wolff (Space Science Institute); **pages 20–21:** Reta Beebe, Amy Simon (New Mexico State Univ.), and NASA; **pages 22–23:** NASA, ESA and G. Bacon (STScI); **page 23, inset:** NASA Kennedy Space Center (NASA-KSC); **pages 24–25:** © Pekka Parviainen/Dembinsky Photo Assoc.; **page 26:** © Eckhard Slawik/Photo Researchers, Inc.; **page 29:** © Eckhard Slawik/Photo Researchers, Inc.; **page 30, inset:** Andrea Dupree (Harvard-Smithsonian CfA), Ronald Gilliland (STScI), NASA and ESA; **page 30:** © John Bova/Photo Researchers, Inc.; **page 31:** McDonald Observatory; **pages 32–33:** NASA Jet Propulsion Laboratory (NASA-JPL); **page 33, inset:** courtesy of the NAIC-Arecibo Observatory, a facility of the NSF; **pages 34–35:** ASA/CXC/SAO; **page 35, inset:** NASA/CXC/SAO; **page 37:** NASA; **page 37, inset:** NASA; **pages 38–39:** NASA, ESA, and Martino Romaniello (European Southern Observatory, Germany); **pages 40–41:** top: NASA, ESA, S. Beckwith (STScI), and The Hubble Heritage Team (STScI/AURA); bottom: NASA and The Hubble Heritage Team (STScI/AURA); **pages 42–43:** Nigel A. Sharp, REU program/AURA/NOAO/NSF; **page 45:** top: NASA; bottom: Carolyn Russo; **page 46:** NASA, ESA, S. Beckwith (STScI), and The Hubble Heritage Team (STScI/AURA); **page 47:** Reta Beebe, Amy Simon (New Mexico State Univ.), and NASA.

1 2 3 4 5 6 7 8 9 10 ✤ First Edition

contents

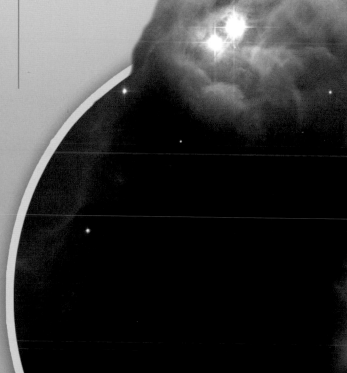

Many of the photos in this book were taken by the Hubble Space Telescope. The colors of the Hubble photos are not always the real colors of the things being photographed. The Hubble uses color as a tool to show certain things about objects more clearly. The Hubble cameras don't use film. They actually use electronic sensors that take pictures in black and white. The colors are added later.

Enjoy these amazing photos of the universe around us. But remember that if you take a rocket-ship ride, the colors you see when you visit space may be different than what you see in this book.

What is a star?

Go outside when it's dark one night
and look up at the stars.
They seem small and calm and
quiet. But if you could see one up
close, you'd be **surprised**.

These stars are very old and
very far away in a cluster
of galaxies called M15.

Stars are **giant** balls of fire.

You've probably seen fires that burn wood or coal. A star burns gas—mostly a gas called hydrogen. You can't see or smell or taste hydrogen, but there is a lot of it on Earth and in outer space. Inside stars, hydrogen can get so hot that some of it changes to another type of gas— helium. Tremendous amounts of energy are released when this happens. This energy becomes light and heat.

Most stars are too far away for us to feel their heat. But one star is not. The closest star to Earth is the sun. The sun's heat is one important reason that life exists on Earth.

A close-up of the nearest star, our sun.

Are most stars like our sun?

The sun is 860,000 miles across—a hundred times as wide as Earth.

A **million** earths could fit inside it.

It burns at about 10,000 degrees Fahrenheit. No oven or fire on Earth could get that hot. The sun shines as brightly as 4 million million million million hundred-watt lightbulbs. (That's a 4 followed by 24 zeros.)

The sun is a medium-sized star, not huge and not tiny. Most stars are cooler and dimmer than the sun, but some are far bigger, brighter, and hotter.

There are stars so big that a billion of our suns could fit inside. And there are stars even smaller than Earth. Some stars can be 10 times as hot as our sun. Some are so cool that they don't even shine. But all stars begin the same way.

SMITHSONIAN LINK
See the life cycle of a sun-sized star online at the Harvard-Smithsonian Center for Astrophysics.
http://sao-www.harvard.edu/seuforum/opis_tour_sun.htm#

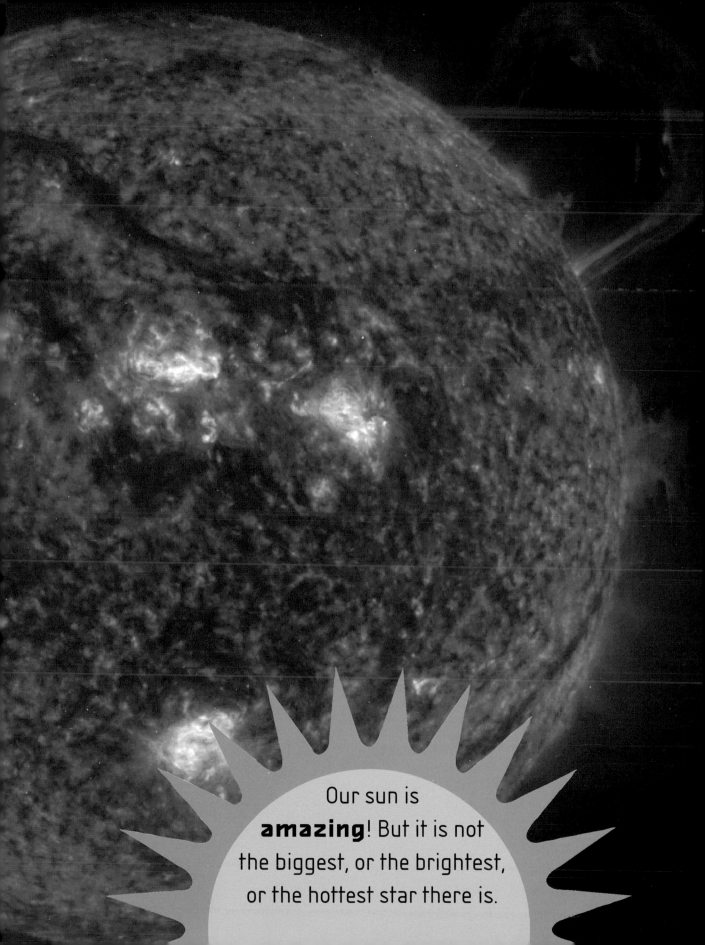

Our sun is **amazing**! But it is not the biggest, or the brightest, or the hottest star there is.

Huge clouds of dust and gas swirl through space. A cloud like this is called a **nebula**. Grains of dust and tiny bits of gas inside the nebula bump into each other. Some stick together. Slowly, over millions of years, the clump gets bigger and bigger. And the bigger an object is, the stronger its **gravity** becomes.

Gravity presses hard on the gases in the center of the clump. The tighter the gas is squeezed, the hotter it gets, until it is hot enough to change hydrogen into helium.

A **star** has been created.

Scientists think that about 275 million new stars are created every day. Even though they all start the same way, they can still be very different from each other. For one thing, not all stars are the same color.

The Cone Nebula, a huge pillar of gas and dust, is a place where stars are born.

How are stars created?

Strange twisted clouds can be seen in the Lagoon Nebula, another star-forming region.

In the middle of this spiral galaxy are mostly older yellow and red stars. Bluer, younger stars are in the outer spiral arms.

Why are stars different colors?

Tiny white dwarf stars, the oldest in our galaxy, can be found in this detail of the cluster called M4.

A flash of light from this ancient red supergiant is lighting up the dust at the edge of our Milky Way galaxy.

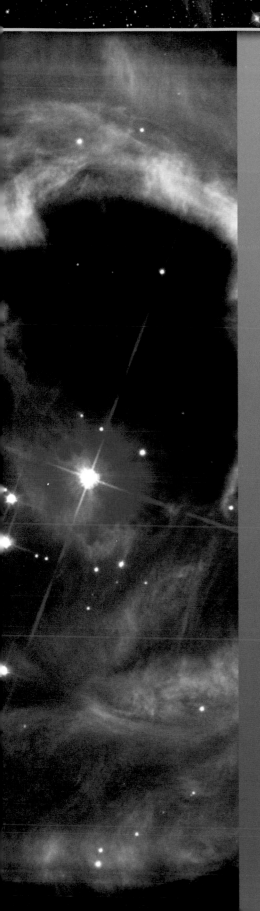

Get an adult to help you light a candle and look at it in a dark room. The coolest part of the flame, farthest away from the wick, is orange or reddish in color. The warmer part of the flame, closer to the wick, is white or yellow. And a tiny blue spark of very hot flame is at the tip of the wick.

Stars are the same way. The hottest stars (which are very big) have a bluish-white color. They are sometimes called blue giants. Medium-sized stars, like our sun, are a little cooler and burn with a yellow flame. The coolest stars are dim and red. Small stars like this are called red dwarfs.

SMITHSONIAN LINK
If you are in Washington, D.C., pay a visit to the Albert Einstein Planetarium at the National Air and Space Museum for a panoramic view of stars of all colors and sizes.
http://www.nasm.edu/visit/planetarium/

There are more **red dwarfs** in the universe than any other kind of star.

Eta Carinae is the brightest known star in our galaxy. It is a dying supergiant.

What's a red giant? What's a red supergiant?

A star the size of our sun will probably burn for about nine billion years. Then its fuel—gases like hydrogen and helium—begins to run out. It starts to cool down, and it starts to get bigger. It has become a red giant.

In about five billion years, our sun will become a red giant. It will be so big that it will swallow up Mercury, Venus, and Earth.

Bigger stars than our sun become red supergiants when their fuel starts to run out. If you could replace our sun with a red supergiant, it would not only swallow up Earth one day, it would reach out as far as Jupiter.

A billion of our suns could fit inside a **red supergiant**.

The red supergiant star at the center is about 20,000 light-years from Earth. This same star is on page 11 in a photo taken a few months after this one.

Red giants and **supergiants** are near the end of their lives as stars. Soon all their fuel will be gone, and they will begin to die.

Red dwarfs are small, but not all red stars are small. Some are huge, many times bigger than our sun. They are called red giants.

The pink blob in the middle is all that's left of an exploded star— a supernova.

What happens when a star dies?

Some stars can burn for only 1 million years. Others can burn for 10 billion and more. The larger a star is, the faster it burns up its fuel, and the shorter its life will be.

After a red giant's fuel is used up, it collapses into a tiny star, a white dwarf. Our sun will end its life as a white dwarf about 5 billion years from now.

White dwarfs can be even smaller than Earth, but they are so **dense** and heavy that a teaspoonful of one would weigh close to 2,000 pounds—more than an elephant.

Stars big enough to turn into red supergiants do not become white dwarfs when all their fuel runs out. A big star like this explodes in a supernova.

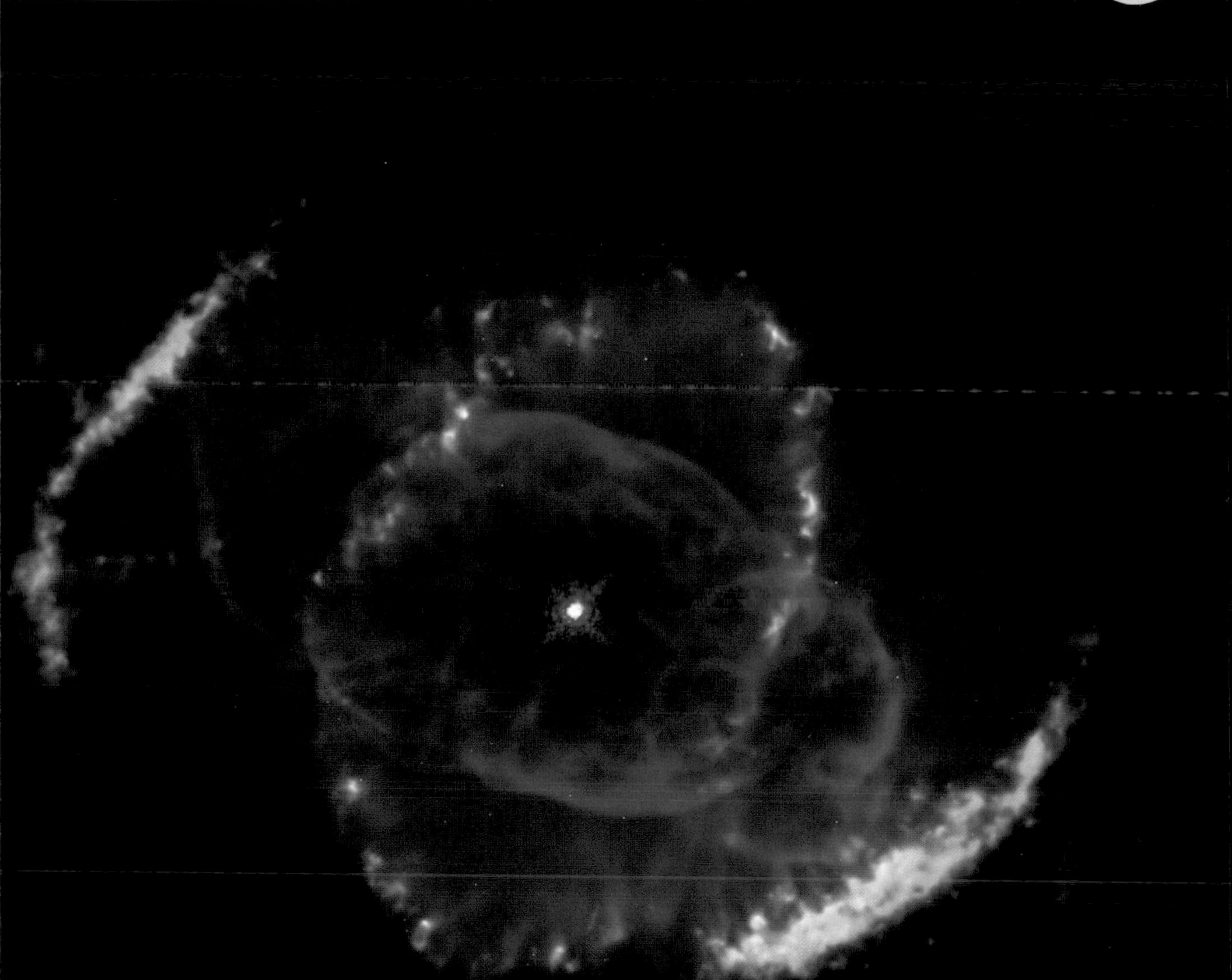

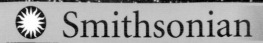

What is a supernova?

What is a black hole?

The faint glow is where a supernova exploded 3,000 years ago.

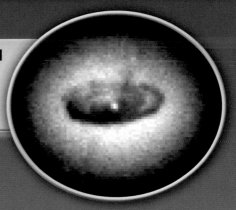

Scientists believe the pull of gravity from a black hole formed this Frisbee-like disk of cold gas.

For a short time, a single supernova can shine as brightly as a hundred billion ordinary stars.

Supernovas are **rare**.

In our galaxy—the huge group of stars that includes our sun—only one might happen in a century.

When a star turns into a supernova, the center of the star does not explode with the rest. It is crushed by gravity into a very small, very heavy ball. The bigger the star was, the stronger its gravity is. If its gravity is so strong that nothing at all—not even light—can escape from it, then the object is called a black hole. This might seem like the end of the star. But the star isn't quite finished.

We can't see **black holes**, but sometimes we can tell that they are there because of the way their gravity changes the nearby planets and stars and nebulae.

Why are stars called the "factories of the universe"?

When stars die, the dust and gases that once made up their outer layers drift into space. Slowly, over billions of years, they begin to gather together into clumps. Some of these clumps will grow big enough to form new stars. Some of them become planets.

Almost everything on Earth—water, dirt, trees, mountains, animals, people, your family, **you**—is made from stuff that was once inside a star.

These young stars are forming from the clouds and dust scattered by wind and radiation from Eta Carinae, one of the biggest stars in the Milky Way galaxy.

At least nine planets, including Earth, orbit our sun. The planets and everything else that circle around a star are called its **solar system**. Planets are much smaller than most stars. Even the biggest planet in our solar system, **Jupiter,** is only one tenth as wide as the sun. Planets do not create their own light, like stars do. They reflect the light of the star or stars closest to them. We can see the planets in our solar system because the light from the sun bounces off them.

Mars is the fourth planet from the the sun. It's called the red planet.

   Do other stars have planets? Some do. We know about more than 150. But because we are so far away from them, we can't see them. Right now, we can tell they are there only by measuring the pull of their gravity on the stars they orbit.

Scientists have **not yet** found a planet—or moon— like Earth that has living things on it.

But there are many, many stars that may have planets. So we keep looking for planets and other things in a star's solar system.

SMITHSONIAN LINK
Learn more about the planets in our solar system by clicking on the Center for Earth and Planetary Studies of the National Air and Space Museum.
http://www.nasm.si.edu/ceps/research/research.cfm

Do all stars have planets?

In the next **ten** years scientists hope they'll be able to take a picture of a planet in another solar system.

Jupiter is the fifth planet from the sun and the largest one in our solar system.

What is in a solar system besides a star and its planets?

In this artist's view is the planet Pluto and, to the right, its moon, Charon.

moons are also part of a solar system. Moons are smaller than planets, and they orbit around planets instead of around stars. Earth has one moon. Other planets may have 2, or 8, or more than 20, or none at all.

Asteroids and comets also orbit around stars. Asteroids are chunks of rock that are too small to be called planets.

If a small piece of rock from space falls into Earth's **atmosphere,** it becomes a meteor. It falls so quickly through the air surrounding Earth that it heats up and burns, making a long trail of light through the sky. If a piece of the meteor makes it all the way to the ground, it is called a meteorite.

It's easy to tell stars from all these other objects in the sky.

Comet Hale-Bopp crosses the skies above the southern United States. Comets are balls of dust and ice. When they pass close to the sun, some of their ice melts, and dust and bits of gas are pushed out into space to form long, streaming tails.

Only stars look like they're **twinkling**.

Why do stars twinkle?

Actually, they don't. But when we see them from Earth, they look as if they do.

The light from the stars must pass through Earth's atmosphere to reach our eyes. When the light hits the air, it is bent a tiny bit one way, then another way. This makes it look like the star is twinkling.

The light that is reflected off a planet must also pass through Earth's atmosphere. But because the planets in our solar system are so much closer to us than the stars, they seem brighter. With the brighter light, the twinkling is much harder to notice.

People all over the world look up every night at the **twinkling stars**. But they don't always see the same ones.

Stars twinkle in the night sky.
The faint streak is a meteor.

Compare the drawing with the bright stars in this photo of the constellation Orion, the hunter. You can clearly see two stars that mark his shoulders and the three stars in a row that make the hunter's belt. The big blue star in his knee is Rigel, one of the brightest stars in the sky.

What's a constellation?

Long ago, people noticed certain patterns of stars that seemed to make pictures in the heavens. People gave names to these groups of stars and told stories about them. We call these groups constellations. There are 88 of them in the sky.

When the ancient Greeks looked at the stars that make up Orion, they saw a hunter. People in other places saw different things in the same group of stars. Some saw an octopus, a cayman (a large reptile like an alligator), or a canoe.

As the year goes by, the **stars** and **constellations** seem to move across the sky.

In North America, you can see Orion in the winter. South of the equator—the imaginary line around the middle of Earth that separates the northern and southern halves of our planet—people see different stars and different constellations. The Southern Cross, for example, is a constellation that can be seen only from south of the equator.

Earth is moving so that we see different constellations at different times. But there is one star over the northern half of Earth that does not seem to move.

What is the North Star?

The North Star, or Polaris, seems to stay in one place all year long. None of the stars really move across the sky. But because Earth's North Pole points directly at Polaris, this star seems to stay still as Earth turns, while the rest of the constellations spin around it.

Whenever people long ago looked at **Polaris**, they knew they were looking north.

You can find the North Star by looking for the group of stars called the Big Dipper. Look at the two outer stars that form the Dipper's cup. Imagine that you can draw a line between these two stars, and follow that line from the bottom of the cup to the top and then straight out into the sky. It will point at the North Star. Because of this, the two stars on the Dipper's outer edge are called the Pointers. The name of the bottom star is Merak and the top star is called Dubhe.

Long ago, people used the North Star to help them find their way. They may not have had good maps or compasses to show them direction.

SMITHSONIAN LINK
Find the locations of stars and constellations by going to the Smithsonian's Astronomy page and clicking on the Galactic Navigation link.
http://www.si.edu/science_and_technology/astronomy/

North Star

The Big Dipper is really the tail and back of the constellation called the Big Bear, or Ursa Major. A straight line connecting the two stars in the outer edge of the dipper points at Polaris, the North Star.

This star in the constellation Orion is named Betelgeuse, from the Arabic words meaning "arm of Orion."

An amateur astronomer looks through a small telescope.

Through an ordinary telescope, Sirius is the brightest star in the northern sky.

Who gets to name the stars?

Polaris is one star that has a name. (It means "pole star.") Over the centuries, people have given names to many stars. We still use these names today. Sirius means "scorching," and it is an old name for the star that looks brightest from Earth.

On a clear, dark night, you can see about **3,000 stars** from Earth just by looking up.

When people began to use **telescopes,** they discovered that there were many more stars—far too many to name them all.

Many stars now just have numbers. The first planets that were discovered outside of Earth's solar system orbit a star called B1257+12. And some stars, like Kruger 60A or Barnard's Star, are named after the scientists who discovered them.

SMITHSONIAN LINK
Have you found something new in the sky? Maybe it will be displayed at the National Air and Space Museum! Be part of the Smithsonian's First Light program for amateur astronomers at:
http://www.nasm.si.edu/exploretheuniverse/firstlight/index.htm

Check out the latest images from the Chandra X-ray Observatory by going to the Smithsonian's Science and Technology page: http://www.si.edu/science_and_technology/

Who studies the stars and how do they do it?

Scientists who study the stars are called astronomers. They use many different tools in their work. Some look at the stars and take photographs through telescopes. Some telescopes use visible light (the kind you can see). Others use kinds of starlight that our eyes can't see. Some astronomers listen to the **radio waves** rippling out from many stars. Some study light and measure other kinds of energy created by stars. Astronomers try to figure out how far the stars are from Earth, how old they are, and what they are made of. They look for planets orbiting other stars.

The biggest telescopes on Earth are built on mountains where the air is thinner and the view of space is clearer. The famous Hale Telescope is on Palomar Mountain in southern California.

The Hubble Space Telescope isn't anywhere on Earth. It is in space, orbiting 380 miles above Earth so the atmosphere will not get in the way of the pictures that it takes. The Hubble Space Telescope can look at stars trillions of miles away.

SMITHSONIAN LINK
Use your own telescope to study space on the Internet. Go to the Smithsonian's Astronomy page and click on the MicroObservatory link: http://www.si.edu/science_and_technology/astronomy/

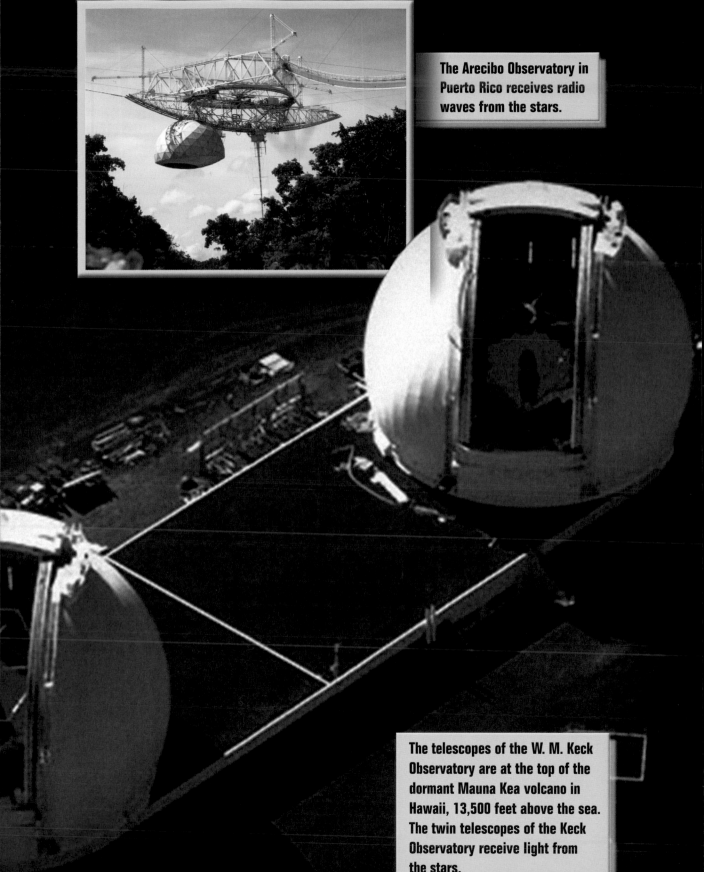

The Arecibo Observatory in Puerto Rico receives radio waves from the stars.

The telescopes of the W. M. Keck Observatory are at the top of the dormant Mauna Kea volcano in Hawaii, 13,500 feet above the sea. The twin telescopes of the Keck Observatory receive light from the stars.

How far away are the stars?

Proxima Centauri is a little more than four light-years away from **Earth**. That means the light from this star takes a bit more than **four years** to get here.

The brightest star in this infrared photo is Proxima Centauri. Traveling 10 miles a second, it would take you 70,000 years to get there.

Proxima Centauri is a red dwarf star.

The sun is the closest star to Earth. But it's still pretty far away: 93 million miles. Imagine you had a spaceship that could travel at 10 miles per second—that's 36,000 miles an hour. It still would take you about three and a half months to reach the sun. But compared to the other stars, the sun is a next-door neighbor.

The stars are so far away that measuring the distance to them in miles is hard because the numbers are so big. (It's like measuring the height of the Empire State Building in inches.) So scientists don't use miles. They use light-years.

If you turn on a lamp, the light travels so quickly from the bulb to the walls of the room that you can't see it moving. But it does move. It moves 186,000 miles a second, or almost 6 trillion miles a year.

That's a **light-year**.

What do astronomers mean when they talk about "looking back in time"?

Proxima Centauri isn't bright enough for you to find in the sky. But if you had a telescope, you could see the light that this star gives off. Remember, though, that light took four years to make it from the star to Earth. That means you wouldn't see the light that the star is giving off right now. You'd see the light it gave off four years ago. So you'd be looking at what Proxima looked like then.

When you look at the **sun**, you're seeing the light it gave off about **eight minutes ago**.

When we look at other stars that are very far away from Earth, we're seeing the light they gave off millions of years ago. The Hubble Space Telescope has taken pictures of stars that are 12 billion light-years away. By looking at very distant stars, we can see what they were like—and what the universe was like—billions of years ago. It's like looking back in time.

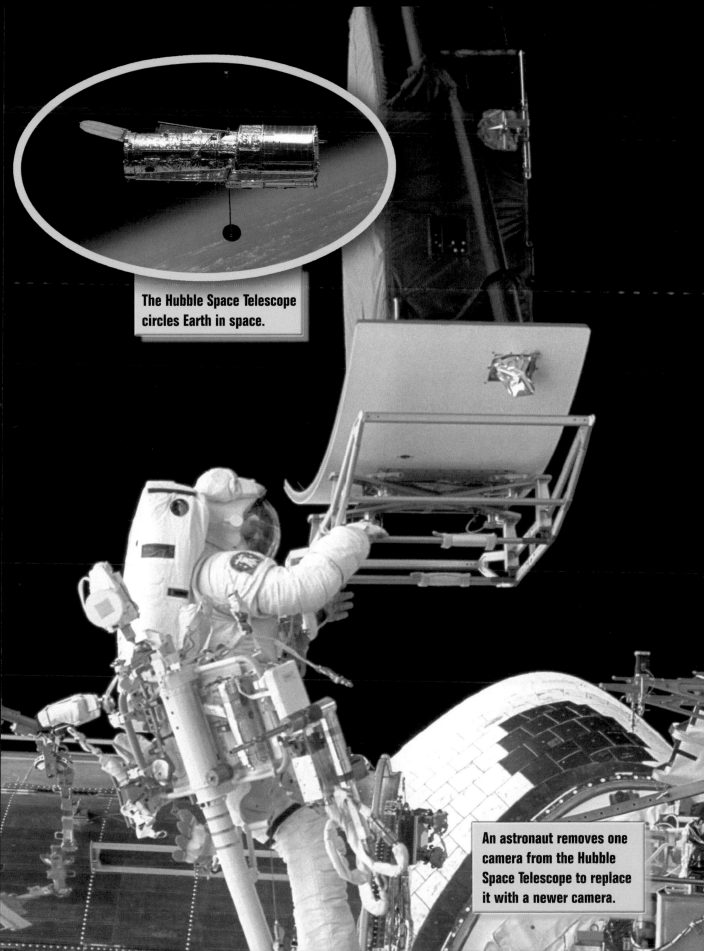

The Hubble Space Telescope circles Earth in space.

An astronaut removes one camera from the Hubble Space Telescope to replace it with a newer camera.

Is each star alone in space or do stars form groups?

Most stars don't float by themselves in the emptiness of space. Stars gather together in groups called galaxies.

The **Milky Way** galaxy has about **200** billion stars.

These stars (and their planets, moons, comets, and asteroids) all swirl around the center of the galaxy.

So you may feel like you're sitting still right now. But you are actually sitting on a spinning planet that is orbiting around a sun that is circling around the center of the Milky Way. You're moving much faster than you thought—more than 500 miles a second!

About 2,000 stars are packed tightly into the Arches cluster in our Milky Way galaxy.

Our **sun** and the planets that orbit it, including Earth, are part of the **Milky Way galaxy**.

The Whirlpool galaxy is spiral-shaped and looks like a pinwheel.

Are there different kinds of galaxies?

The shape of this galaxy has been twisted by a collision with another galaxy.

Some galaxies are big, some small. Some are shaped a little like a Frisbee with a bulge in the middle, with long, curving arms that trail out into space. These are called spiral galaxies. The Milky Way is shaped like this. Other galaxies are round like balls or eggs or even flattened out to look like cigars. And some galaxies are blobs, with no clear shape at all.

Stars gather together in galaxies, and galaxies gather together in groups or clusters. A group has a few galaxies. A cluster has hundreds.

All the galaxies together make up the universe. The universe is our name for everything that exists—the stars, the planets, you, your little brother, your school, your neighborhood, asteroids, comets, and nebulae, and even empty space with nothing in it. The universe is everything there is.

And the **universe** is full of stars.

SMITHSONIAN LINK
Visit the National Air and Space Museum's "Explore the Universe" exhibition online at:
http://www.nasm.si.edu/exhibitions/gal111/universe/etu/index.html

There may be about 10 billion trillion stars in the part of the universe that we can see. If you started at one and counted a number every second, it would take you 30,000 years to count to a trillion. You'd need to do that 10 billion times to count how many stars there are.

Imagine that you are holding a grain of sand between your fingers. Now imagine that grain of sand getting **bigger**. . . and **bigger**. . . until it's **bigger** than Earth itself, big enough to be a star. Now imagine every grain of sand on the beach getting to be that big. This isn't close to the number of stars in the universe. There are more stars than there are grains of sand on every beach and in every desert in the entire world.

Some of those stars have planets. Maybe somewhere, on a planet circling a distant star, someone is wondering how many stars there are in the universe.

Just like **YOU** are doing **RIGHT NOW!**

How many stars are there?

Light pours from the center of a cluster of galaxies called M22 with more than 10 million stars.

Ask the Specialist

Sean O'Brien

When did you become interested in astronomy?

I've been interested in what things are, where things are, and how they work for as long as I can remember. I've been interested in astronomy from early on because I'm interested in the stars, the planets, and all the other wonderful things "out there."

What do you do most of the time?

Actually, most of my day is spent supervising, as I am one of three operations supervisors for the Albert Einstein Planetarium and Lockheed-Martin IMAX Theater at the National Air and Space Museum. The astronomy-related work I do is educational, but I also do research to check my facts.

What are the most important qualities for an astronomer?

Curiosity and patience.

What kind of education do you need?

My current work requires a bachelor's degree.

Do you need any special training (apart from a college education) for your job?

There is much on-the-job training to do my job, and I had to teach myself some things, like using a telescope.

What new technology has helped you most with your job?

Computers, computer networks, and the resources available through the Internet.

What do you like most about your job?

We meet a wide variety of people of all ages and backgrounds here. The National Air and Space Museum is the most visited museum in the world.

What is the biggest recent discovery in astronomy?

I have to choose?! I am personally fascinated by the wonderful images and other measurements about Saturn, its rings, and its many moons, returned from the *Cassini-Huygens* spacecraft. It's amazing!

like planets around other stars (if any such planets exist).

What is the most important unanswered question in your field? Do you think you will ever be able to answer it?

I find it difficult to choose one question. "Is there other life in the universe other than here on Earth?" is one such question. As to its answer, I do not know when or if positive proof will be found.

How can kids get interested in astronomy?

As star gazer Jack Horkheimer says, "Keep looking up!" The best way to start learning about astronomy is to start learning your way around the night sky. No telescope required.

Is there something in your field you wish everyone knew about?

There are so many things! I like the concept contained in Carl Sagan's sentence in *Cosmos*: "We are made of starstuff." For those old enough to know something about chemicals, the carbon, oxygen, nitrogen, and other elements that make life possible, that make *us* possible, are created in massive stars near the end of their lifespan. The chemicals are released into space when the stars explode as supernovas and are recycled to make new stars and new planetary systems. The sun and Earth were formed in this way. Our bodies are made from these materials in the soil, water, and air. We are made of starstuff!

Is there anything that you think astronomers will be able to do in the future that they can't do now?

I look forward to the day when telescopes will be able to directly observe Earth-

Glossary

atmosphere–the layer of air or gas that surrounds Earth or another planet or moon

dense–tightly packed together or compressed

dormant–not active, but may become active again. *A dormant volcano has not erupted in a long time and will probably not erupt soon.*

gravity–the force that attracts or pulls objects together

Jupiter–the fifth planet from the sun and the largest in the solar system. It is about 484 million miles away from the sun, nearly five times as far away as Earth.

nebula–a cloud of gas or dust in space. Plural: nebulae

orbit–to travel around an object in a regular, circular path

planetarium–a complicated projector that shows the movements of the stars, planets, and moons on a curved ceiling

radio waves–long energy waves found throughout the universe and used on Earth to carry signals to radios, televisions, and cell phones

telescope–an instrument that views distant objects. Also, any instrument that observes the stars and space, like a radio telescope, which receives radio waves from space.

Places to Visit

Go to a Planetarium

To find out more about the stars, the solar system, space travel, and much more, visit a planetarium or a science museum in your area. With movies, exhibits, games, and activities, museums are the next best thing to traveling in outer space!

For a list of sixty-six first-rate planetariums, see:
www.google.com/Top/Science/Astronomy/Institutions/Planetariums/North_America/United_States

Websites

There are links to many wonderful web pages in this book. But the web is constantly growing and changing so we cannot guarantee that the sites we recommend will be available. If the site you want is no longer there, you can always find your way to plenty of information about the stars and a great learning experience through the main Smithsonian website: www.si.edu.

http://starchild.gsfc.nasa.gov/docs/StarChild/StarChild.html
This site by NASA has lots of information about stars, planets, and the universe.

http://antwrp.gsfc.nasa.gov/apod/astropix.html
Visit this site for a new outer space picture every day.

http://coolcosmos.ipac.caltech.edu/cosmic_kids/AskKids/index.shtml
Ask an astronomer a question and look up the questions other people have asked.

http://sao-www.harvard.edu/seuforum/blackholelanding.htm
Visit a black hole at the Harvard-Smithsonian Center for Astrophysics.

http://spaceplace.nasa.gov/en/kids/
Find games, activities, and experiments about stars and space.

http://webdbnasm.si.edu/whatsnew/index.cfm
Get all the latest information from the major observatories on Earth.

http://sao-www.harvard.edu/seuforum/missions.htm
Find dozens of satellites and telescopes looking into space.

Suggested Reading

Astronomy, by Rachel Firth

A Child's Introduction to the Night Sky, by Michael Driscoll

Destination: Space, by Seymour Simon

Out-of-This-World Astronomy: 50 Amazing Activities & Projects, by Joe Rhatigan

Zoo in the Sky, by Jacqueline Mitton

Index